THINGS SOCIAL WORKERS Really WANT TO Say But Can't

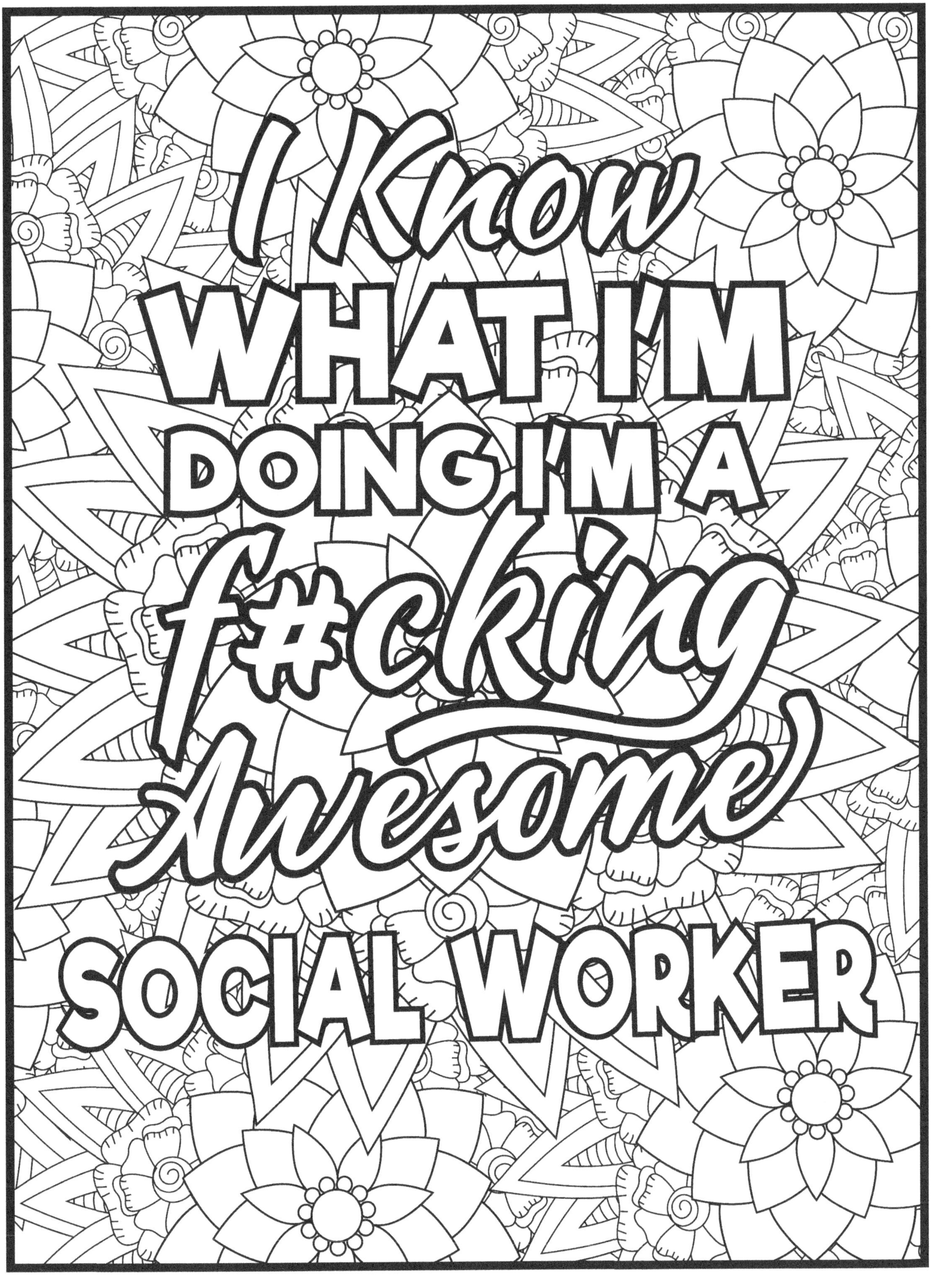
I Know
WHAT I'M
DOING I'M A
f#cking
Awesome
SOCIAL WORKER

KEEP
CALM
&
CARRY
THE F#CK
ON

Happiness
IS AN
INSIDE
job

I'm A
SOCIAL WORKER
Not a
Fucking
MAGICIAN

I Can &
I FUCKING
Will

BELIEVE IN
Your Own
CREATIVE
POWER

be Happy
EVERY
damn
DAY!

Be the Light
You're amazing

You Are
Made Of
MAGIC

Keep
Life
simple

I PLAY
WITH
MY F#CKING
RULES

Hey, you're
FUCKING
Great

LIFE IS SHORT
SMiLE WHiLE YOU
STiLL HAVE TEETH

friday
IS MY
SECOND
Favorite
F-WORD

THAT AIN'T
MY FUCKING
Problem

fucking
great
SOCIAL WORKER

Too Calm
TO GIVE A
Damn

DON'T MAKE ME
USE MY
SOCIAL WORKER
VOICE

INHALE
Courage
EXHALE
Fear

Calm The
F*ck
Down

Smile More.
Worry
Fucking
Less!

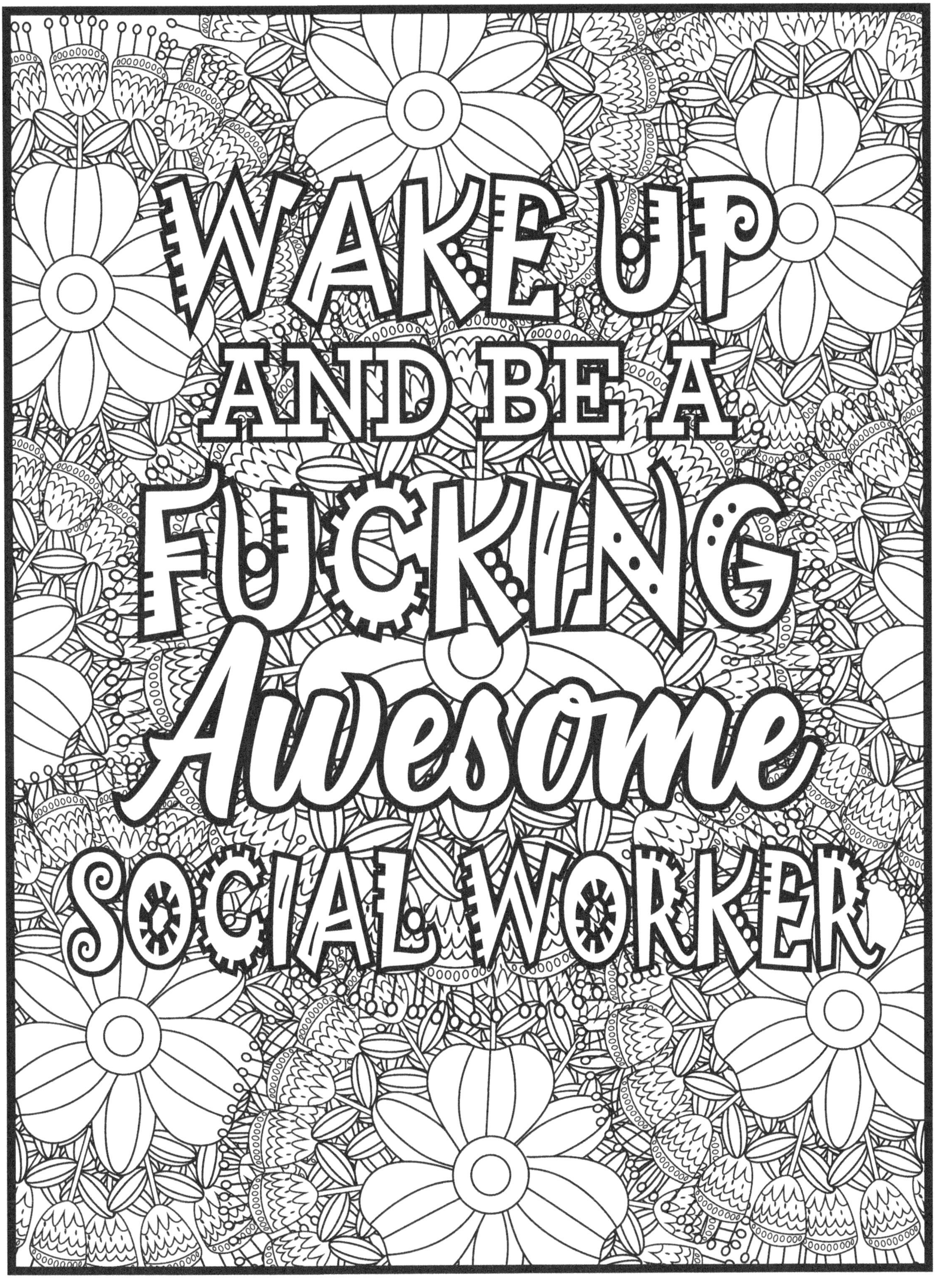
WAKE UP
AND BE A
FUCKING
Awesome
SOCIAL WORKER

You Are
Fucking
Adorable

Spread Love
EVERYWHERE
YOU FUCKING
GO

I'm Not
DOING
THAT
Sh*t

CALM THE
F#ck Down
&
Color

You Are
A FUCKING
Rock

I'm Worthy
of happiness
And love

DON'T
COMLPAIN
JUST
F#CKING
DO IT

I'm a nice
Person
Just don't
push my
bitch button

HUSTLE
LIKE A
SOCIAL WORKER
LIVE LIKE
A LEGEND

LET THAT
SH*T
GO

Why Don't
You Fucking
Do it

POWERFUL
GRATEFUL
AND READY TO
FACE THE
WORLD

Every Day
Is A Fresh
Start

WORLD'S
Okayest
SOCIAL WORKER

I'm A Kind
OF A
FORKING
GREAT
Deal

I Gave
Zero
Fucks
Today

Test Your Colors

THANKS FOR CHOOSING Our COLORING BOOK.
WE TRULY HOPE THE RECIPIENT OF THIS
BOOK GETS A FEW LAUGHS FROM THE QUOTES INSIDE.
AS A SMALL BUSINESS SELLING ON AMAZON,
YOUR FEEDBACK IS IMPORTANT TO US. WE WOULD
APPRECIATEIT IF YOU COULD tAKE A MINUTE TO POST
AN HONEST REVIEW ON AMAZON.